SCALE MODEL AIRCRAFT
from
Vac-form Kits

Hugh Markham

Gresham Books

Published by
GRESHAM BOOKS
Unwin Brothers Limited
The Gresham Press
Old Woking
Surrey GU22 9LH

ISBN 0 905418 34 4

Typeset by Reproprint
Leatherhead, Surrey.
Printed in Great Britain by
Unwin Brothers Limited
The Gresham Press
Old Woking
Surrey GU22 9LH

Some idea of the potential of vac-form kit modelling is given in this view of a fine 1:72 scale replica made by the author of the elegant Elizabethan-Airspeed's Ambassador — used by BEA in the fifties and still serving the independents in the seventies. A Contrail kit is used to make this model.

Contents

Two models which further illustrate the varied and unusual models available as vac-form kits. **Top:** *The McDonnel XP-67 Bat.* **Above:** *Fokker G1 Reaper. The Reaper uses the technique mentioned in the text whereby the fuselage is moulded in transparent acetate and the picture shows how well this suits an aircraft model which has a large area of glazing. Models by Rareplanes in 1:72 scale.*

Introduction

Before discussing vac-form modelling it is esssential to dispel the myth that this presents greater difficulties than would be encountered with an equivalent injection moulded kit.

To the serious modeller, prepared to devote time and care to his, or her hobby – and which of us is not? – vac-forms offer challenge and variety as the photographs illustrating this book show.

What is vacuum forming? As applied to model aircraft it is a method of forming shapes in plastic sheet by the application of heat and the exhausting of air. The creation of this partial vacuum causes the heat softened plastic sheet to adopt the shape of the mould over which it is placed. Vac-form kits are not sold in all hobby shops. In fact, you'll mostly find them with the specialist mail order suppliers or direct from the makers. Look in model magazine adverts for sources of supply.

In this book the aim is to provide the basic information needed for building, detailing and finishing vac-form models. The simplicity of the techniques to be described will show that the modeller who has gained experience from assembling injection moulded kits has available, in this medium (vac-form), a wide and diverse range of interesting subjects.

These chapters will briefly state the contents of a vac-form kit (and touch upon those items not supplied); advise on tools and materials; explain the preparatory work required; relate the step-by-step construction; show methods by which existing detail may be improved and added to. They will survey the products of the principal manufacturers (with notes on variations of style and detail), and provide some reference to retail suppliers of vac-form kits, materials, decals and tools.

As an example of the relatively simple and straightforward construction essential to any first attempt, the Rareplanes Seafire 47 is cited in the instructional phases of these pages. This kit not only meets this requirement but combines with it the ability to produce a superb model of a hitherto unobtainable subject. If

Made by Contrail is the graceful Short Singapore III flying boat, greatly enhanced by correct rigging and a perfect finish. It is typical of exotic aircraft types not available as conventional plastic kits, but sold by specialist suppliers as vac-form kits.

you can't find a Seafire kit – vac-form models have limited production runs – find an alternative of similar low wing configuration for a first attempt.

It is virtually certain that any reader of this book will have reasonable experience of making up conventional injection-moulded polystyrene kits. With this in mind I have *not* included chapters dealing with references, research, painting, markings and displaying, since procedures in these aspects of model making are no different from conventional kit building. It goes without saying, however, that all remain equally essential and important, the research aspect probably more so. In this book you'll find only passing reference to these matters but, of course, they cannot be omitted from the overall modelling activity.

1: The Vac-form Kit

Generally the vac-form kit consists of one or more moulded plastic sheets containing all the major components (fuselage, cowlings, wings, tailplanes, etc.). Most kits now incorporate wheels and spinners on these sheets. A number, notably Rareplanes, include many smaller details such as propeller blades, separate gear doors, seats, floor and instrument panels, drop tanks and similar ancillary equipment. Where they are needed, moulded transparencies are provided though these, because of difficulties inherent in moulding transparent styrene, are usually formed in PVC. Nearly all kits contain adequate information for assembly. Airframe (of Canada), Contrail (from Sutcliffe Productions) and Rareplanes always supply good, scale, three-view drawings. The two latter companies augment this with

The Rareplanes 1:72 scale Lockheed Vega is another model featuring a fuselage in transparent acetate so that when the model is painted the windows form a realistic flush fit to the fuselage.

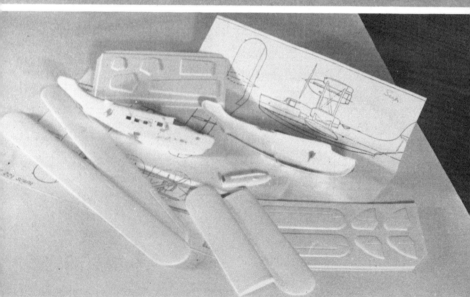

Top: *This is what a vac-form kit looks like — sheets of moulded components, in this case for a Contrail model of the TSR-2 in 1:72 scale.* **Above:** *Early stages of making up a Contrail kit of a Supermarine Scapa. Some parts have been separated from the sheet and the fuselage windows on one side have been cut out.*

exploded diagrams, comprehensive instructions and details of colour schemes.

Not supplied are gear legs, finished propellors, wing struts for biplanes, and decals. There are, however, exceptions – Sutcliffe Productions have included some of these items in their recent Contrail releases (and say they intend to extend this policy): their kit of the Russian AWACS aircraft, the Tupolev Tu-126 (Moss), and that for the Tu-20 have excellent injection moulded main gear legs and contra-rotating propellor assemblies. Both these kits include good quality decals, again a provision that the makers say will be continued.

In the larger Rareplanes kits these parts appear, beautifully moulded, on the vac-formed sheet and, providing they are used as the instructions suggest, function admirably. Airmodel kits now include a random selection of spinners and struts (injection moulded) which, although necessitating some compromise, are useful. Airframe too have included decals. Their delightful kit of the Heston Napier Racer is much enhanced by the inclusion of the specialised markings.

Packaging and presentation is fairly uniform. Whilst the majority are bagged in polythene, the very large kits, requiring extra protection, are stoutly boxed. A wrapper or box label gives details of the contents; on this Contrail and Rareplanes usually feature a photograph of the finished model.

2: Tools and Preparation

A well equipped tool kit is of great benefit to all aspects of modelling; care in selection will not only ensure that the most useful aids are available but will also avoid other heavy expense. The basis of any model workshop must be the work board. Choose one having a close grained surface similar to that of a chopping or bread board. A size of 18 ins by 15 ins gives a cutting line, on the diagonal, of about 24 ins and will accommodate all but the largest of models.

Also required will be a craft knife – a pen type handle with separate blades is recommended; fine (razor) saw – a handle is not essential; a selection of (Swiss) needle files – round, flat, oval and square; fine cut rat-tail files – 1/8 ins and 1/4 ins diameters; pin chuck (Eclipse pin vice No. 121) – 1.0 mm/0 – .04 ins) and a stock of 1/32 ins and 1/64 ins twist drills (more of the former); graduated set of twist drills from 1/16 ins to 1/4 ins; straight edge or steel rule; dividers; pointed and chisel ended tweezers; 'wet and dry' abrasive paper – 240 grade for rough work, 400 for intermediate and 600 for finishing.

Cements – adhesives – fillers

For bonding vac-formed styrene parts a thin, methyl ethyl keytone (MEK) based liquid cement is used for almost all joins (the exceptions will be dealt with later). It is also used as a surface restorative prior to painting. Apply (to joins) with a size 0 or 00 brush.

As the cockpit canopies and other moulded transparencies are produced in a dissimilar material to the styrene either a PVA, impact, or cyanoacrylate glue is utilized. If the last named is used please be sure to heed the warnings.

Rareplanes from time to time use transparent acetate to form small cabined fuselages (where cut-out windows would cause weakness), and acetone is the agent used here. Mating styrene parts such as wings or tailplanes to the acetate will require one of the adhesives previously specified for joining dissimilar materials.

Various fillers are available; Green Stuff, a proprietary American brand of green filler (available in the UK), though slightly more expensive, can be thoroughly recommended; mention can be made of car body fillers such as Brummers Waterproof Stopper, but the choice, in the end, must be a personal one.

Materials

White plastic card (styrene sheet) .005 ins and .010 ins thicknesses; transparent plastic card .010 ins and .020 ins; 1/4 ins masking tape used not only when painting but also to bind parts together while joins are drying out. The tape is also used to mask-off the edges of areas where filler is being applied.

Scrap off-cuts from the kit should be retained for use when making wing spars and other structural parts. Models with tricycle gear will need lead shot and Plasticene for the nose weight. Assorted sizes of this shot can be purchased from fishing tackle shops.

Futuristic in its day was the Westland-Hill Pterodactyl. Kit by Airframe is in 1:72 scale. Though delicate work is needed to make the undercarriage, the wings and fuselage of this model are very simple to assemble.

Above: *Magnificence in 1:72 scale – the Rareplanes version of the Douglas DC-4 Skymaster is a large and impressive model. Note the well-moulded panel and rivet detail.*

Below: *The futuristic Bell Airacuda prototype of 1940 with unconventional layout. This is also by Rareplanes.*

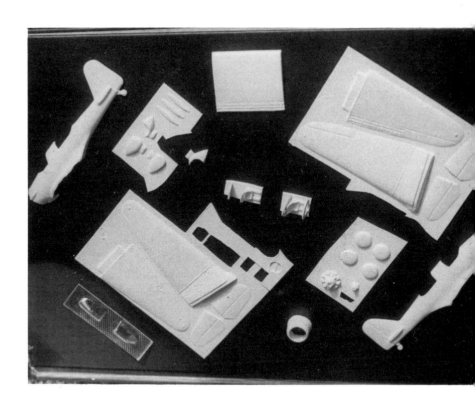

Above: *First phase with a Rareplanes kit. Parts are shown being separated from the sheet.*

Below*: The method of opening slots, windows, etc., as described in the text. First stage is to drill corners, as can be seen in the right hand of the three windows below. The middle window is partly cut out and the left hand window is complete.*

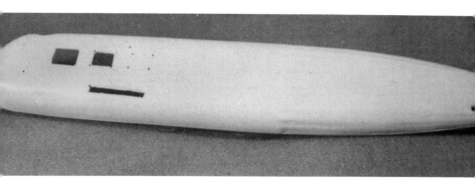

Paints

When considering the painting of your model it cannot be repeated too often that one or two really good brushes (properly looked after) will do far more towards achieving a satisfying finish than a large selection of inferior quality. An air-brush is a useful, if expensive, luxury that should in no way be regarded as replacing the paint brush but only as a helpful adjunct. Brush sizes to meet most contingencies would include Numbers 00, 2 and 5.

All the paints you require will be contained in one or other of the ranges available from your model shop. Specific colours can usually be obtained by inter-mixing *within* a range. Always have a plentiful supply of white spirit available. It is very much cheaper if bought by the gallon or half gallon; use it for cleaning up, brush washing and paint thinning (check paint instructions). Make sure the paints you choose are suitable for use on plastic.

Pre-construction

Having looked at the tools, materials and paints helpful to the vac-form modeller we can move on to the preparatory work needed prior to assembly. Carefully examine the contents of the kit, identify each of the moulded shapes and, from the drawings, sketches and instructions, recognize where they will fit.

Use the craft knife to separate the items from the moulded sheet. It is not necessary to cut right through the plastic; a sharply scored line, made as close to the subject as possible, will suffice, the surplus plastic can then be snapped off. Practice this 'score and snap' method on some scrap material – it will be found satisfactory even when the line followed is eccentric.

When the pieces have been cut from the sheet there will be seen to be, around the edges, a small radius or lip caused by the transition from the flat sheet into the moulded shape. Remove this lip with a needle file of appropriate shape, using the tool at such an angle as to avoid damage to any surface detail.

On those parts which will be joined together to make complete components (fuselage halves, top and bottom wing panels, nacelle halves, wheel halves, etc.) the mating faces need to be made smooth and true. This operation should be undertaken with care and with constant reference to the scale drawing to avoid the removal of too much material. A centre line marked on the fuselage plan view will make easier the checking of the two halves.

The method advised for this stage is to place, on a *flat* surface (it *must* be *flat* – a sheet of glass is ideal), a sheet of medium grade 'wet and dry' (for very large parts in heavy gauge plastic a coarser grade can be used). Using plenty of water to reduce the risk of tearing, commence 'sanding' the mating face. Exerting a steady pressure and working slowly with a circular movement (this ensures even removal), proceed until satisfied, by checking against the drawing, that the desired finish has been attained. When all the items calling for this work have been completed care must be taken to avoid subsequent damage.

The various apertures – intakes, windows, wheel wells and the like – now have to be made. The method for all these is simple and similar only varying to encompass the differing shapes. Small openings for intakes are drilled (either 1/32 ins or 1/64 ins dependent on size) and then brought to finished contour with the tip of a round or rat-tail file. Circular windows, camera ports (as in the port and starboard rear fuselage of the Seafire 47) and round landing lamps are drilled just under full-size and completed with a round file. Rectangular openings are drilled 1/32 ins at each corner and the drill holes then joined with a knife cut – this is a 'roughing' stage and should leave the hole under size. Finishing is effected by the use of the most suitable shaped files. Wheel wells are also made in this way although it may, if the shape is awkward, be necessary to divide the area into two or more sections.

Where cockpits are located across the fuselage join they require a slightly different technique. The hole is firstly roughed out with the fine saw and craft knife; the two fuselage halves are offered together and the opening marked for matching. The cockpit is then trimmed to size (various files) but at the 'front and rear, where the two shells meet, just enough surplus material is left on to allow for final matching when the fuselage has been assembled.

If the mainplane consists of separate port and starboard wing panels (as on the Seafire) it will be seen that each of these components has two parts (top and bottom) making four mouldings in all. On each of these, between the root end leading and trailing edges, at right angles to the inner face, there is a web of moulded plastic. Carefully cut and file this away. Do not, at this point, trim the wing panels to length. Inspect all the parts for burrs or ragged edges and, where necessary, smooth off with medium and fine 'wet and dry' paper.

Details such as propellor blades which have a shaped front and reverse face will need, due to the limitations of the forming process, filling and shaping. Add the filler as soon as the part has been cut out and cleaned up, but leave the shaping until the item is required for assembly thus allowing the maximum time for the filler to cure.

Boulton Paul Sidestrand; medium bomber forming equipment of 101 Squadron from 1928 to 1934 when it was succeeded by the Overstrand. The Contrail kit from which this model was made will produce either aircraft.

The Mayo Composite. Imperial Airways experimental combination of the late 'thirties. Power at take-off of the lower component was used to augment range of the upper. Maia flying boat by Contrail; Mercury seaplane by Airframe, both to 1:72 scale.

3: Model Assembly

In the previous pages the necessary preparatory work was described; we shall now consider the manner and method of assembly. As already mentioned, because of its simplicity, these notes have been written with the Rareplanes Seafire 47 in mind. However they are not intended to be specific but rather to have a general application to the assembly of all small vac-form models.

Begin by cementing the pilot's seat to the cockpit floor; fashion a control column from stretched sprue, drill the floor to accept this, and then cement it in position. Cement the instrument panel and the floor/seat assembly into the starboard fuselage half. Cut eight small tabs approximately 3/8 ins long by 1/16 ins wide from .005 ins plastic card and cement them, at intervals, around the edges of the starboard fuselage shell. They should project about 1/32 ins to form locating keys for the port half.

Now we come to the glazing of the camera ports (one in each half), as these are less than 1/4 ins in diameter there are at least three ways in which this can be done. The moulded transparencies supplied in the kit can be used, fixed in place with either PVA, impact or cyanoacrylate adhesive (if the latter, heed the warnings); discs of .010 ins transparent plastic card can be cut – use the hole in the fuselage as a template – and cemented in position with liquid cement or (and it is believed that this is the most satisfactory method for small apertures) they can be ignored until the model is finished and painted and then treated, following the instructions on the bottle, with Kristal Kleer, an American proprietary product available in the UK.

The cockpit furnishing that has been suggested is obviously of the barest nature and many modellers will want to add more; if this is your intention now is the time to do it.

With .010 ins plastic card blank off the chin intake; add strips of .010 ins plastic card behind (inside) the exhaust stubs. Paint, as necessary, the cockpit fittings and the insides of both fuselage halves.

Offer up the two shells and, when satisfied that they are

correctly located, bind them together with 1/4 ins masking tape. After re-checking the location, carefully 'flood' the join with liquid cement. To avoid the cement running and causing surface damage it will be found helpful to apply masking tape lengthwise along the fuselage 1/8 ins either side of the join. When the cement has thoroughly dried out (allow at least 12 hours) remove the binding and touch in with cement those areas previously obscured. After the join has completely hardened off it should be cleaned up with medium and fine grade 'wet and dry' paper adding, if needed, filler. Any surface detail lost during this process can be re-indicated by careful use of the craft knife. Again it is suggested that the risk of such damage can be minimised by masking off the edges of the work area.

Carefully trim the canopy to a snug fit over the cockpit then use one of the quoted adhesives for dissimilar materials to glue it in place. 'Wet and dry' paper (medium grade, finishing off with fine) wrapped round a rod or dowel of similar diameter to the upper fuselage cross section will be found helpful in attaining the close seat essential. Complete this task by filling any gaps and smoothly blending in. Open up the exhaust stubs using drill and file tip and taking care not to dislodge the blanking plates fitted inside.

Before assembling the wing panels provision must be made for fitting the undercarriage. For this, on the inside of both wing top mouldings, mark the point of leg attachment and on these marks cement a plastic block 3/16 ins square and 1/8 ins thick (if you do not have this thickness available it can be made up from several laminations). In each block drill a 1/32 ins hole – a pilot hole which will be opened up later to accept the leg – taking care not to drill so deep that you break the outer surface of the wing. Appearance will be improved if all the corners are rounded off. Cement together the top and bottom mouldings for both wings – as with the fuselage the parts can be held in place with masking tape until the cement has dried, whereupon the same process for cleaning up can be used.

The tailplane is assembled in a similar manner but this unit will, as it is moulded all in one piece, need to be cut into two separate, port and starboard, component parts. Use the fine (razor) saw for this operation.

The next stage is the mating of these five major sub-assemblies, ie, fuselage, port and starboard wing panels, port and starboard tailplanes. Before starting this prepare, as you would for an injection moulded model, supports for the wings and tailplane

Above: *This sleek Supermarine Seafire FR47 is from a Rareplanes vac-form kit and is ideal for any newcomer to this type of modelling. It is one of the simplest on the market.* **Below:** *This is how a Rareplanes kit is supplied; a neat sheet of mouldings and an excellent scale drawing with colour scheme data.*

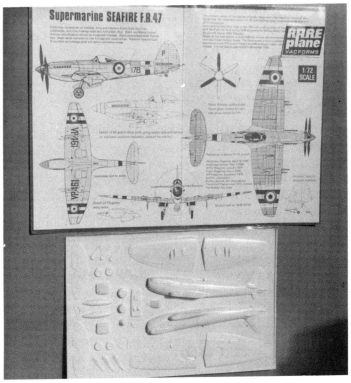

during assembly; these can be simple cardboard jigs or just blocks of the requisite height – obviously the method chosen will be that to which you are most used.

After making sure that both tailplanes are correct to the drawing and that the root ends will butt well against the fuselage, cement on to the root rib moulded on each side of the tail. Check for alignment and support while the join dries.

At the root end of each mainplane trim away any surplus until the length and fit are right to the drawing and to the fuselage stub wing. Whilst doing this remember to allow for the dihedral angle; more material needs to be removed from the upper surface than from the lower. It is worth taking extra trouble at this stage as the better the fit between the wing panel and the stub wing the stronger will be the resultant join. Cement the wings in position paying particular care, in all three planes, to the alignment. Set the dihedral angle, arrange the supports and leave, at least overnight, to set.

Apply filler to the wing/fuselage and tailplane/fuselage joins, once again making use of masking tape to contain the filler within the desired perimeters. Smooth off and blend in, using small sections of 'wet and dry' and, working gently, avoid damage to the adjacent detail. Thoroughly inspect the completed airframe and, if satisfied that all necessary cleaning up has been done, brush liquid cement *lightly* over the whole structure (other than the transparencies) to restore the surface of the plastic.

Cement together the two halves of both wheels. From stretched sprue make the two undercarriage legs allowing, in their length, for the attachment within the wing. With tip of a file ease open the pilot drilled mounting holes – note that on the Seafire the legs are raked both forwards and outwards. Cement in place the two legs, the undercarriage doors and, having smoothed off the joins, the wheels. Use the drawing to confirm that these parts all have the right 'sit'.

Try the rear propellor hub against the fuselage nose and, if necessary, 'sand' to a good fit; in turn, check and adjust the front hub against the rear and the spinner against the front, blending all three parts into a smoothly flowing line. With fine 'wet and dry' paper carefully complete the shaping of the six propellor blades – these having been filled and set aside during the preparatory phase. Make up the contra-rotating airscrew assembly as shown in the kit drawing and then cement to the nose of the fuselage.

Join the two halves of the auxiliary fuel tank; make its supports from scrap plastic card then cement the completed unit and the two radiators onto their respective locations. Lightly brush liquid cement over all the parts that have been added.

Drill the wing leading edges, where indicated, to accept the four cannons; under the port wing drill a 1/32 ins hole for the pitot mounting; drill the tail fairing for the arrester hook and the fuselage top decking for the whip aerial. Make all these details and the small tubular structure forward of the tail wheel from stretched sprue. If you have a well equipped spares or bits box you may already have available some of the smaller items mentioned; for example the legs, wheels and pitot head from the Airfix Spitfire might be used, whilst the propellor from the same kit could provide at least part of the Seafire assembly

Your experience will guide you in the painting of the model. Sufficient here to remind of the necessity to make sure that any filled areas are adequately sealed and to mention the colour scheme and the paints needed. The Seafire 47 wore the standard post-war Royal Navy finish – extra dark sea grey (Humbrol HB.7) upper surfaces; sky (HB.5) side and under surfaces. The aircraft depicted in the kit drawing carried Korean War (UN Forces) black and white identification stripes. The requisite 'D' type roundels are fairly readily available in a number of transfer ranges. Identity and serial numbers will be found on Model-decal sheets numbers 33, 34, 35 and 36 (obtainable from Modeltoys, Portsmouth) a source which will also supply the four-inch 'Royal Navy' titles for the rear fuselage.

A suggested method of achieving the overall sheen typical of British military aircraft of the early 1950s is to apply a light coat of well thinned satin finish polyurethane varnish, this will also give excellent protection to the applied transfers. The paint should be allowed at least a week in which to dry out before laying on the varnish.

When building Airframe (Canada) kits the cutting and fitting of the location tabs can be omitted. This manufacturer includes in his kits a moulded keel member which serves the same purpose.

Internal structures – strengthening members

For the larger vac-form model some internal strengthening is advisable – most kit manufacturers recognise this and, where necessary, make mention of it in their instructions usually giving suggestions as to how and where it should be incorporated. Many kit drawings actually show where these stiffening members should be located. Some kits include parts for this purpose on the moulded sheet, whilst others supply printed patterns which have to be traced on to spare plastic card.

Generally the requirement is for one or two wing spars (depending on the size and span of the model and thickness of the plastic used in moulding) and a number of formers and panels in the fuselage. Panels will also be needed as mountings for the gear units. These will want reinforcing with extra thicknesses of material where they are drilled to accept the gear legs and struts. As the wing spars provide not only span-wise stiffening but also help to spread the load when the model is standing on its undercarriage some thought must be given to achieving interconnection between spars and gear mounting points. Fuselage formers should be so located that they form an anchorage for the wing spars. Where these details are not provided as mouldings there is usually enough off-cut material left over from the kit to cover their manufacture.

For models with a nose wheel undercarriage it is necessary to make provision for the stowage of nose weight. Often a box for this purpose can be built below the cockpit floor and above the nose wheel bay in to which can be loaded lead shot packed in Plasticene. Do ensure that such boxes have side walls which prevent the Plasticene being in actual contact with the inside of the fuselage shells as such contact can sometimes cause softening of the plastic. The photographs show several aspects of the structural methods described.

If neither patterns nor parts are provided for the fuselage formers the following method of establishing their shape is suggested. Soft wire – 18 swg is ideal – is pressed into the shell to produce a template. Alternatively plasticene can be used in place of the wire.

Biplane Assembly

The wing assembly of a biplane will be made easier by the use of simple jigs. Some kits, notably Contrail, provide patterns for such aids; where they are not supplied they will need to be made utilising the information contained in the scale drawing, and using dividers to establish the extent of the gap and stagger between upper and lower wing. The length of the interplane (but

Truly unusual as a model subject in 1:72 scale is the massive Contrail kit of the Soviet Air Force's Tupolev Tu-126 Moss AWACS aircraft. The spinners and propellors come ready moulded in hard plastic in the kit, taking care of the most awkward part. Below is shown fuselage internal structure.

not the centre section) struts can be gauged at the same time. An example of this type of support jig is illustrated, as is the method of utilisation (see page 27).

Draw the parts for the jigs (or trace the patterns) on to stout card; carefully cut out the various pieces, remembering that you will need two of each to make a port and starboard jig; glue parts together using an impact adhesive – no great strength is required in this bond. Cut and trim to length the interplane struts using strips cut from scrap plastic card and shaped to an aerofoil section or, in the case of those kits which now include such items,

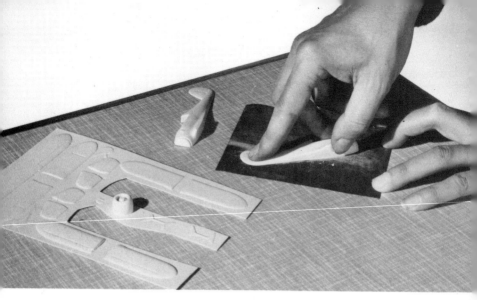

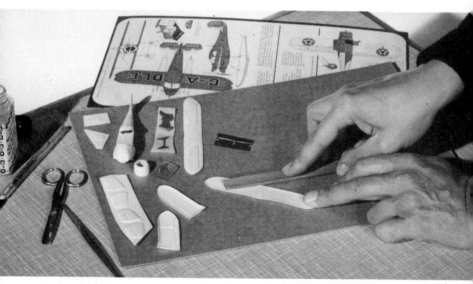

Top: *Fuselage halves have been cut from the kit sheet and are given smooth butting edges by careful and even rubbing with a slight circular movement on a sheet of 'wet and dry' paper. A perfectly flat work surface (here a Formica-covered table) is essential.* **Above:** *Using an emery board or fine file to rub down the slightly rounded edges formed in the wing by the vac-forming process. An even butt is essential on all wing edges. Note work board and bottle of MEK (at left) used for cementing the parts.*

the injection moulded parts. In either case leave a small mounting peg at each end.

Make up the kit to a stage where the lower wing is attached to the fuselage and the upper wing is assembled ready for mounting. Make sure the strut locations are drilled out and will accept the strut pegs. Place the jigs on the lower wing, one port and one starboard, locating them so that they do not obstruct fitment of the struts. Place upper wing in position on top of the two support jigs, check alignment, then bind the structure together with masking tape. After again checking alignment cement the interplane struts into their respective locations. Leave the assembly, preferably overnight, to thoroughly dry out. Cut to length the centre section (cabane) struts, again using the dividers to ascertain dimensions. Cement struts in place and leave to thoroughly dry out.

Carefully remove the binding tapes and gently slide the jigs sideways to clear the struts and then tilt until they can be eased out from between the wings.

Rareplanes Vindicator – a re-tooled re-issue of their earlier 1:72 scale kit.

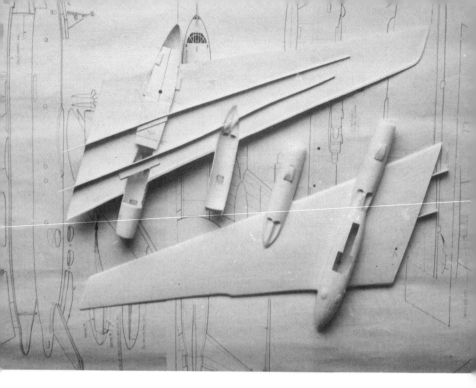

Above: *Tu-126 wing structure – note how rear spar is interlocked with gear mounting.* **Below:** *Internal structure for a medium size model. Fuselage formers, flight deck, noseweight box and nosewheel bay can be seen in this Contrail Airspeed Ambassador.*

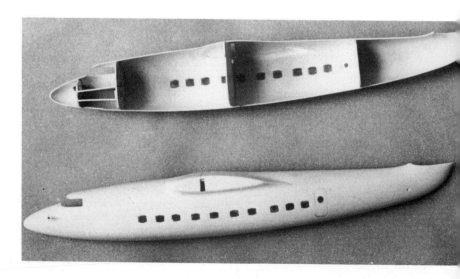

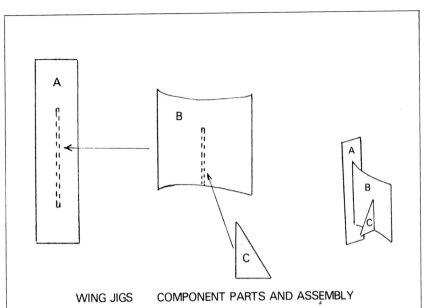

WING JIGS   COMPONENT PARTS AND ASSEMBLY

See text, page 23.

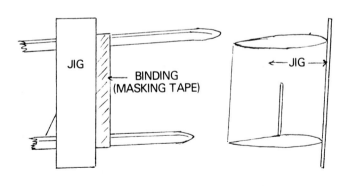

JIG

BINDING
(MASKING TAPE)

← JIG →

WING JIGS   METHODS OF USE

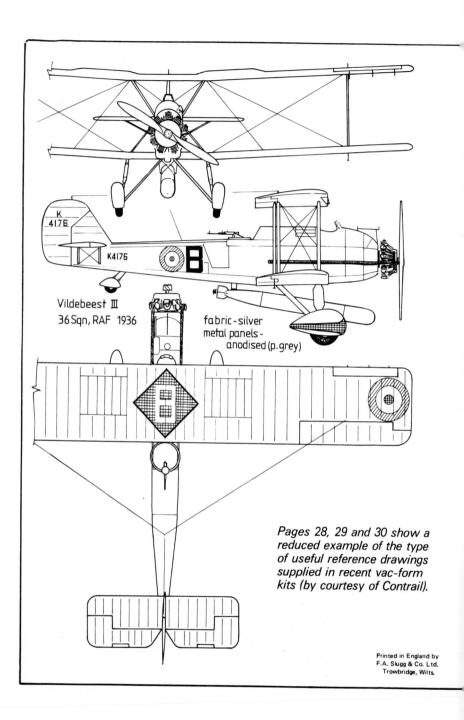

Vildebeest III
36 Sqn, RAF 1936

K
4176

K4176

fabric-silver
metal panels-
anodised (p.grey)

*Pages 28, 29 and 30 show a
reduced example of the type
of useful reference drawings
supplied in recent vac-form
kits (by courtesy of Contrail).*

Printed in England by
F.A. Slugg & Co. Ltd.
Trowbridge, Wilts.

VICKERS VILDEBEEST/VINCENT

REFERENCE MATERIAL

AIR CLASSICS VOL 5 NO 3 FEB 1969
BOMBER SQUADRONS OF THE R.A.F.
BOMBERS OF THE R.A.F. SINCE 1914   PUTNAM
VICKERS AIRCRAFT SINCE 1908   "
AIRCRAFT OF THE R.A.F. SINCE 1918   "
BOMBERS BETWEEN THE WARS 1919- 1939   BLANFORD
ENCYCLOPEDIA OF WORLD COMBAT AIRCRAFT SALAMANDA

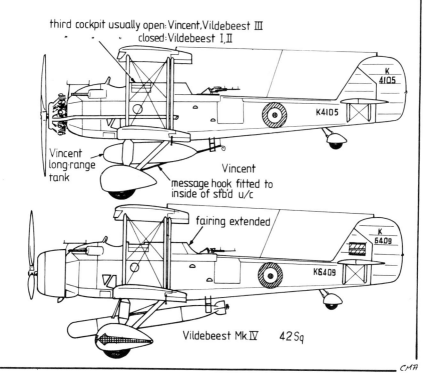

third cockpit usually open: Vincent, Vildebeest III
"   "   " closed: Vildebeest I, II

K4105

Vincent long·range tank

Vincent
message hook fitted to inside of stb'd u/c

fairing extended

K6409

Vildebeest Mk.IV   42 Sq

CMA

29

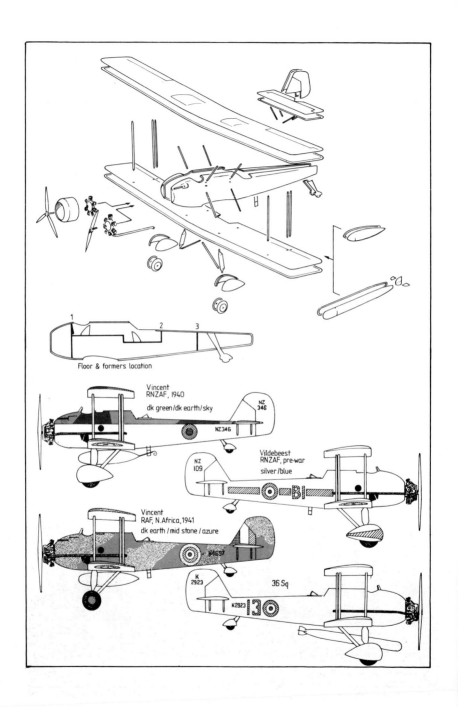

Floor & formers location

Vincent
RNZAF, 1940

dk green/dk earth/sky

NZ
346

NZ346

Vildebeest
RNZAF, pre-war

silver/blue

NZ
109

BI

Vincent
RAF, N.Africa, 1941

dk earth/mid stone/azure

K4697

K
2923

36 Sq

K2923 130

4: Adding Detail

Adding extra detail, or enhancing that which already exists, has almost unlimited possibilities and its extent, whether internal or external must depend on one's personal requirements. It can well be regarded as a specialised subject within its own right and the modeller wishing to explore it in greater depth can be given no better advice than to obtain and study the Almark publication *Painting and Detailing Model Aircraft* – a clear and lucid guide written by an expert in this field, Les Whitehouse.

However, some notes of a more general nature are valid here. Although the importance of photographs as a means of reference has been widely stressed it cannot be repeated too often. Try to find pictures of the specific aircraft being modelled. When the opportunity arises to photograph interesting subjects do not be content with only the usual side, front and three-quarters views, but aim to include close-up shots of particular areas such as gear

The type of detail photograph, taken at an air show, which is always of value for model making. This shows the intakes, ducts, and lights in the wing of a Nimrod.

The type of 'close-up' that can aid the detail addict. Hendon Museum's Stranraer. Note the mooring bollards, hatch cover and grab rails. If you are making a model of the Stranraer this picture will be invaluable. But try to find as many photos as you can — and drawings — for any model you make and study them closely to get the 'atmosphere' of the real thing.

Above: *The mainplanes and tailplane of this Saro London show examples of the use of stretched plastic card tapes, in this instance as representing the rib-fabric attachment tapes.* **Below:** *The nacelle of a Singapore shows how details, made from scrap, can be added to enhance the appearance. The rigging and control wires are made from various thicknesses of stretched sprue. This is a 1:72 scale model but looks remarkably real from this angle!*

legs, intakes, markings, etc; these can provide an invaluable source of information.

The quality and quantity of surface detail in the moulded parts varies considerably between one range and another – even between one kit and another – and the degree to which it needs to be improved or augmented is largely determined by this variation.

Obviously the ideal condition would be where surface marking is to such a high standard as to require no enhancement. If the manufacturer cannot achieve this it would be better, in my personal opinion, to omit it altogether; by so doing a great deal of tedious rectification work could be avoided.

However, when one is faced with poorly moulded and exaggerated lines complete removal, by filling and smoothing, is the only answer. Use a sharp blade in the craft knife (Blade No. 11) to lightly re-incise the erased marks to a sharper definition and deliniation. Similarly, crude raised detail should be eradicated. Here, add filler and reinforcing scrap plastic card to the inside before rubbing down the offending exterior. Cut and contour replacements from scrap or off-cut plastic card.

Strips of plastic card heat-stretched over a lighter or candle flame can be pulled into plastic tape of an infinite variety of widths and thicknesses. These tapes have many uses, indication of longeron and rib positions, fabric attachment tapes, the framing and ribbed surfaces of walkways are some examples; you will find many more. Practice this technique by cutting a number of plastic card strips about 2 ins long and ranging in width from 1/16 ins to 1/4 ins and experiment by stretching under varying tensions and differing heating periods.

5: Conversion Kits

In addition to the many vac-form kits for complete models released in the course of the year a considerable number of conversion sets are issued. These are intended for use in conjunction with an existing injection moulded kit, the combination producing a variation on the the original theme. This variation can be of a comparatively minor nature – a different canopy or an added radome – altering the model only from one Mark to another, or it can involve a major modification in which, say, a vac-form fuselage is married to injection moulded wings and tail.

When using a conversion kit the vac-form parts are prepared and assembled as already described but it must be kept in mind that where, for example, injection moulded wings are mated to a vac-from fuselage, the load applied by the relatively heavy injection moulded components will mean that additional internal bracing is required. In the Vimy Commercial and Vernon models illustrated (Contrail Conversion Kit/Novo Vickers Vimy) four

Classic conversion using a Contrail vac-from fuselage with a Frog/Novo Vimy kit to produce a Vickers Vimy Commercial airliner.

Top: *Vickers Vimy Commercial airliner G-EASI ('Old Go-easy') of Instone Air Transport and later Imperial Airways.* **Bottom:** *Vickers Vernon bomber/transport. Both models use Contrail conversion sets in conjunction with the Novo Vimy kit.*

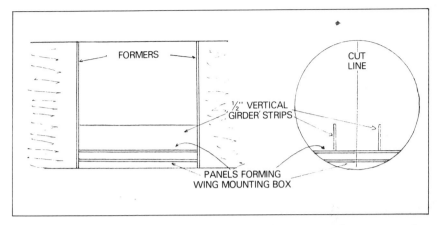

Layout of details for the wing mounting box and for extra reinforcement in the fuselage of the Vimy Commercial airliner/Vernon conversion. Side view and cross section.

fuselage formers are fitted. Between the two in the centre section area are positioned two panels cemented at each end to a former and along the side to the fuselage wall. These form a box into which the wing locating tongue can be fitted. Along the top of this box a 1/22 ins wide strip of plastic card is cemented, like a girder between the two formers, to give further reinforcement. In the instance cited the work was facilitated by first cutting the two relevant formers along their vertical diameters into port and starboard halves, these halves then being cemented into their respective shells. The sketches show the disposition of these parts in the fuselage.

6: Kit Survey

We come now to survey the sources of supply. Although the growing enthusiasm for this type of kit has created a proliferation (both in the UK and the United States) in the number of firms engaged in vac-form production it is, primarily, four houses which dominate the scene.

These are Rareplanes and Contrail in the UK, Airframe in Canada and Airmodel in West Germany. All, through agencies, enjoy a fairly wide international distribution. Each marque has its own particular characteristics reflected in its style, quality and subject choice.

Rareplanes

The model press has been loud in its praise of Rareplanes products; each release confirms that, with quality equal to the

An attractive and colourful Rareplanes offering is the Curtiss A-8 Shrike, US Army attack plane of the 1930s. Model by the author.

Republic P-47N, the final Thunderbolt variant, is from a Rareplanes kit.

very best in injection moulding, this praise is justified. The spectrum of their releases is wide and each one, subject as it is to a limited production run, enjoys the cachet of being a potential collectors item.

If Rareplanes have their sights firmly set on the US market this surely is not to be wondered at and in any case the UK modellers are often compensated by the inclusion of alternative parts for a British variant. The Rareplanes kit of the Boeing YB-17, for instance, contains thirty additional items (including a second fuselage and tailplane) to convert a Revell or Airfix B-17 into a RAF Fortress 1, whilst that for the Douglas DC-4 has extra mouldings for the Merlin engined version.

As well as these and the Seafire FR47, dealt with earlier in this book, the Rareplanes list offers, or has offered, a Lockheed Super Constellation (in either military or civil guise); Bell Airacuda; Fairey Fulmar I/II; Curtiss SBC-3/4 Helldiver; Douglas OP.43 Observation; DH 89a Rapide; North American FJ-1 Fury; Curtiss A-8 Shrike (with radial engined A-12 variant too), and many more, all in 1:72 scale.

A considerable amount of interior furnishing is provided in these kits; crew seats, bulkheads, instrument panels – with the dials, etc, moulded in relief – floors and, in the case of the Rapide, seats, floors and partitions with which to equip the passenger cabin. Except in cases where they would be too small to be practical (and here they would be formed from stretched sprue as described for the Seafire), undercarriage legs are included on the moulded sheet; they are, if reinforced as suggested in the kit instructions, quite a viable proposition.

Drawings, constructional and painting notes, and general presentation, are to a high professional standard and provide information on several alternative colour schemes. Bearing in mind the overall quality, and especially the superb surface definition, of Rareplanes kits one can be thankful that an increasing number of model shops, as well as most of the mail-order specialists, are now stocking this range which can, of course, also be obtained direct from Rareplanes, 69 Redstone Hill, Redhill, Surrey, England.

Airframe

Behind the series of kits marketed by Airframe one can discern the aim of its creator, John Tarvin, to model those aircraft which tend more towards the exotic; add to this his prediliction for the smaller model and you have two factors with which many modellers find accord and which are contributory to the continuing expansion of this catalogue.

It had to be a brave manufacturer who would seek to evoke the frail elegance of the 1913 Taube monoplane. That Airframe succeeded in this was amply confirmed by the model magazine reviews at the time of its release.

The items on offer from Airframe span a broad period of aviation's history; 1913 and World War I (Phoenix D1, Sopwith 1½ Strutter, Siemens Schuckert D111, Morane Saulnier L) to post World War II (DH 108 Swallow), passing some fascinating milestones on the way. The Hansa Brandenburg W20 – a diminutive (in 1:72 scale its wingspan is less than four inches) biplane flying boat; Professor Hill's Westland built Pterodactyl; the mail carrying upper component of the Mayo Composite, the Short four-engined seaplane, Mercury; the Vickers Wellesley and a host of others. To this list has been added the Fairey Long-Range monoplane and A. E. Hagg's Heston Type 5 Napier Racer, the aesthetically pleasing lines of which are very well rendered in this kit that includes transfers for the registration markings. Mouldings in all these kits are clean, sharp and well defined in shape. Surface detail is kept to a minimum, a fact for which, keeping in mind the small size of most of the models, one must be very grateful.

A three-view drawing, construction notes and information as to finish are provided and are usually accompanied by a brief background synopsis of the subject. This is a range from which the author has gained a great deal of pleasure and one which he feels able to unreservedly commend. Most of the Airframe kits are stocked (in the UK) by Ernest Berwick Ltd, of Kettering, whilst the Canadian address is Airframe, 5209 Rumble Street, Burnaby 1, BC, Canada.

Contrail

Somerset-based Sutcliffe Productions (manufacturers of Contrail) have been responsible for some of the most adventurous issues of the past few years. A series marketed as 'Bombers of the Thirties' that included the Sidestrand, Overstrand, Heyford and Hendon was quickly followed by a unique collection of between-the-wars biplane flying boats ranging from the Supermarine Southampton of the late 'twenties to the Scapa and Singapore III of the middle and late 'thirties, an era of fascinating aircraft whose somewhat elusive characteristics are well realised in these kits.

Post-1945 civil aviation is another avenue recently explored by Contrail the Airspeed Ambassador, Miles Marathon and Avro Tudor arriving at the end of 1976 whilst an earlier offering had been a conversion kit for the Avro York.

With this company's noticeable leaning towards the larger subject it is no surprise to find under its aegis kits such as the Blackburn Beverley, Convair B36 (temporarily out of production) and the NA B-70 Valkrie. The Tupolev Tu-126 Moss turboprop airborne radar and command ship (has alternative parts for Tu-114 airliner), the Tupolev Tu-20 Bear and the Myasischev MYA-4 (201 M) Bison have all been released now including excellent injection moulded airscrews and under carriages and also appropriate decals.

Another release, the Supermarine Scimitar, was obviously overdue. This is demonstrated by the fact that at one time recently £16 was being asked in the secondhand market for a

Two from Airframe. **Top:** *The RAF's Fairey Long Range Monoplane used for record distance flights.* **Above:** *The Westland-Hill Pterodactyl MkV, a 2 seat tractor fighter developed from the Mk Ia/Ib illustrated ealier.*

Frog kit, long out of production, of the prototype.

Sutcliffe's have constantly sought to improve the quality and content of Contrail kits. Comparison of current with early releases will show how successful they have been in this. Moulded panel lines on the latest products are of a much finer standard; drawings and instructions are clear and explicit. The addition, as already mentioned, of injection moulded parts removes one of the major problems associated with vac-form modelling and the inclusion of first class transfers disposes of another. The provision of printed patterns from which to make cardboard assembly jigs is another aid, particularly helpful in the construction of the biplane models.

As will be seen from advertisements in the model press many of the mail-order hobby shops now stock Contrail kits. They can be

Above: *The Vickers Valiant in 1:72 scale by Contrails makes an impressive model.* **Below:** *Britain's first post-war commercial airliner was the Avro Tudor, made as a large 1:72 scale model from a Contrails Kit.*

Airmodel Heinkel He 70. The kit – for a military Heinkel He 70G – has been modified slightly to produce this civil Lufthansa version.

obtained direct from Sutcliffe Productions, The Orchard, Westcombe, Shepton Mallet, Somerset, England, BA4 6ER.

Airmodel

A very extensive range emanating from West Germany which includes not only kits for complete aircraft but also many conversion sets. Airmodel output has been prodigous – as many as five or six releases in a month – and, inevitably, this has resulted

Probably the most requested kit in 1:72 scale, the Avro Vulcan, here modelled from a Rareplanes kit.

B-70 by Contrail showing main (fuselage) sub-assemblies standing in front of a finished, painted model.

Supermarine Stranraer in 1:72 scale by Contrail is yet another classic flying boat of the 1930s available in kit form. Stranraers served on into the early part of World War II.

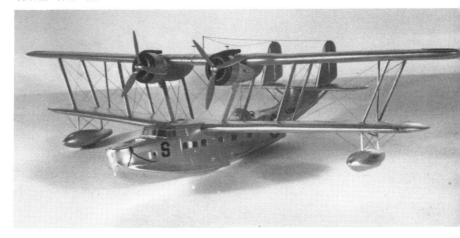

in some variability in quality. The general standard has however been maintained at a fairly high level and has seen some outstandingly good issues; the Do.26 trans-Atlantic flying boat, the Ju 90 airliner and the Northrop Flying Wing all being worthy of particular mention.

One criticism which could justifiably be levelled at Airmodel in the early days related to the poverty of drawings and paucity of information provided. It is obvious that a lot of hard work has been put into remedying this situation and the drawings currently included in the kits are first class.

In good Airmodel issues (and there have been many) the mouldings are clean and well defined with the number of parts, by careful planning, reduced to the minimum thus simplifying assembly. Another welcome feature is the inclusion of an assortment of injection moulded struts and spinners.

Many of Airmodels kits are conversion sets; these fill a very useful role enabling one to ring the changes and escape from restrictions to choice made by the manufacturer of the original injection moulded kit. An example of this type of combined operation is seen in the Vickers Valetta where Airmodel supply a vac-formed fuselage, canopy, etc, and the balance of items required to complete the model come from an Airfix Wellington.

Airmodel kits are readily available, Squadron Shops providing wide distribution in the United States, whilst in the UK Ernest Berwick carries the whole range and BMW hold good stocks. Airmodel Products, 2, Gassentorstrasse, D-7513 Stutensee-Buchig, West Germany.

Formaplane

A comparative newcomer to the market Formaplane offer an interesting list. Commencing at the end of 1977 with the Noorduyn Norseman it now includes the H. S. Nimrod – an outstanding kit which was a winner in the IPMS 1977 championships – the H. P. Hastings and the Russian Mil 24. Mouldings are clean and sharp with reasonably restrained detail. Presentation is good usually including a three-view scale drawing. Obtainable direct from BMW Models (address follows) and various mail-order houses.

Byplanes

A small but superb range of 1/48 scale models. Earlier kits of the Sopwith Snipe and Bucker Jungmann included the propellors, radial engines etc., cast in white metal; subsequent issues for the Yak 3, Polikarpov 1-16 and Meteor F8 have such parts injection moulded. Excellent mouldings carry surface detail of the very highest standard. First class decals and comprehensive instructions plus a scale drawing place these amongst the aristocrats of vac-form kits. Pamela Veal Ltd, Pineacres, Birch Lane, Chavey Down, Ascot, Berks, England, SL5 8RF.

Sundries

As important as knowing what is wanted and what is available is knowing where to get it. A growing number of hobby suppliers are offering specialised services to the vac-form modeller and some of these are listed here.

Ernest Berwick (Leisure) Ltd, 11a Newland Street, Kettering, Northants.

Can supply all tools and materials (such as Green Stuff body putty) mentioned in these pages. Paints by Humbrol and Pactra. Transfer ranges by ESCI, Aerodecals, Blick (Rub-on), Almark. Kits from Contrail, Formaplane, Rareplanes. UK stockists of the Airframe range.

Modeltoys, 246 Kingston Road, Portsmouth, Hants.

Complete and up-to-date range of Rareplanes, most of the Contrail kits. Microscale (1:72 series only), Letraset and Air transfers. Micro system products. Particular attention is drawn to the Modeldecal range of transfers; this, certainly, is one of the two finest ranges in the world and although not specifically designed for the vac-form market many useful applications can be found such as that suggested in the chapter on assembly relating to the serial numbers, etc., for the Seafire. Can only be obtained from Modeltoys.

BMW Models, 327/329, Haydons Road, Wimbledon, London, SW19.

Suppliers of the new Formaplane kits; also stock some by Contrail. Full back-up range of tools, materials, paints and transfers etc.

Aknowledgements

Author and publishers wish to thank Airframe, Contrail, and Rareplanes for supplying some photographs used in this book. Other photographs and drawings are by the author.

Vickers Wellesley Mk I in 1:72 scale is relatively straightforward. It is made from an Airframe (Canada) kit and is in 1938 period finish.

Also Available . . .

SCALE MODEL AIRCRAFT IN WOOD

V. J. G. Woodason

In this age of plastic construction kits there is still a place for the hand-made model in wood. Despite the many kits available there are still hundreds of aircraft types not made in kit form. The answer is to make them yourself from wood. This new edition of an old classic work has been updated to take in recent ideas and developments. It is fully illustrated and outlines constructional techniques in detail, with many practical examples. All model aircraft enthusiasts will find this book useful.

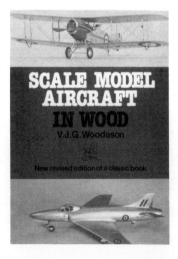

Uniform with this volume